Feb 19

When Sparks Fly

The True Story of Robert Goddard, the Father of US Rocketry

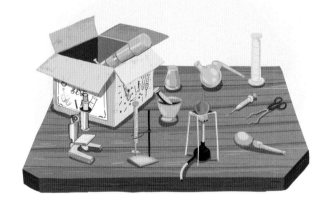

By Kristen Fulton

Illustrated by Diego Funck

MARGARET K. McELDERRY BOOKS
New York London Toronto Sydney New Delhi

MARGARET K. McELDERRY BOOKS
An imprint of Simon & Schuster Children's Publishing Division
1230 Avenue of the Americas, New York, New York 10020
Text copyright © 2018 by Kristen Fulton
Illustrations copyright © 2018 by Diego Funck
MARGARET K. McELDERRY BOOKS is a trademark of Simon & Schuster, Inc.
For information about special discounts for bulk purchases, please contact
Simon & Schuster Special Sales at 1-866-506-1949
or business@simonandschuster.com.
The Simon & Schuster Speakers Bureau can bring authors to your live event.
For more information or to book an event, contact the Simon & Schuster Speakers
Bureau at 1-866-248-3049 or visit our website at www.simonspeakers.com.
Book design by Debra Sfetsios-Conover
The text for this book was set in Calvert MT.
The illustrations for this book were rendered in gouache and acrylic
and were colored digitally.
Manufactured in China
0418 SCP
First Edition
2 4 6 8 10 9 7 5 3 1
CIP data for this book is available from the Library of Congress.
ISBN 978-1-4814-6098-9 (hardcover)
ISBN 978-1-4814-6099-6 (eBook)

To Ben, Jessica, and Hunter:
you are the sparks
—K. F.
To Julen, Otto, and Nika
—D. F.

Special thanks to the Robert H. Goddard Library at Clark University in Worcester, Massachusetts. Their collection of notes, transcripts, and all the actual journals written by Robert Goddard made this story possible. And to Fordyce Williams, who runs the Goddard research archives—her assistance was invaluable.

And to my husband, Rusty, a real rocket scientist. As a fourteen-year-old boy he built a Goddard rocket that ignited his future.

Kristen Fulton

ON A COOL OCTOBER MORNING IN 1882, the tiny town of Worcester, Massachusetts, got a new neighbor.

He was small and pale, but his eyes flashed with a spark of curiosity and discovery.

His name was Robert Goddard.

When Robert was three years old, he learned that he could make static electricity. He dragged his stocking-covered feet across the carpet; the tiny jolt of shock ignited his curiosity.

When it was time to start school, Robert was too sick to go. Many days he found it hard to catch his breath. His lungs felt tight, and with every breath he took, he whistled. The doctor called it wheezing. His parents wanted him to learn, so they gave him a cardboard box full of science equipment.

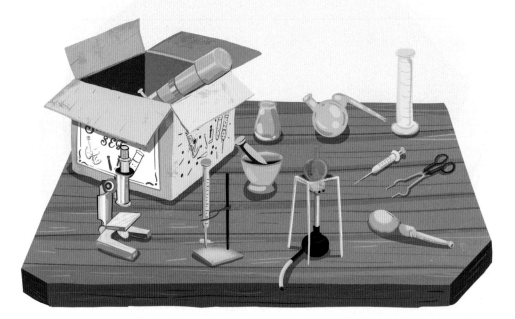

He even got a subscription to *Scientific American* magazine.

Every day, Robert journaled about his experiments. And every week a new magazine arrived full of the latest discoveries.

Robert wanted one of those inventions to be his.

In one issue, Robert read about diamonds. He learned they were made from hardened carbon.

Diamonds and Carbon

The dozens of pencils lining his desk caught Robert's eyes as he read. If pencils were full of graphite and graphite was made from carbon, could Robert make diamonds from pencils?

SCIENTIFIC AMERICAN

NEW YORK, JAN

GRAND CENTRAL STATION IMPROVEMENTS AND TRACK CONNECTION WITH THE RAPID TRANSIT SUBWAY

Robert grabbed his science kit, broke open each pencil, and scraped out the graphite. He emptied a small vial of hydrogen into a pan and added the slivers of graphite. He twisted the knob on the oxygen tank he used for breathing, and a flame flickered under the pan.

The graphite grew hotter.

And brighter.

And BIGGER!

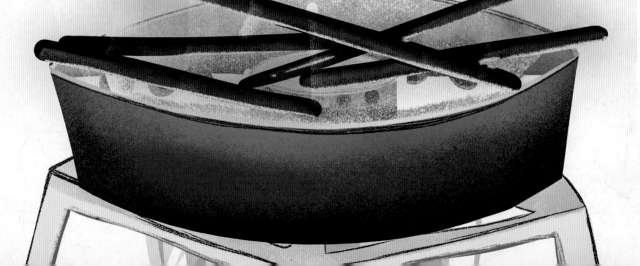

Robert hustled to his desk and scribbled in his journal: Hydrogen and oxygen when combined near a flame will ignite.

His experiment didn't make diamonds, but it wasn't a failure. He learned something . . . explosive!

As Robert grew, so did his curiosity.

One day Robert climbed his
favorite tree to read his favorite book,
The War of the Worlds, by H. G. Wells.
Within the first few pages he was lost
in a world full of Martians and aliens
flying to Earth in giant spaceships.
Robert wondered if he could build
something that would soar to space.

The next morning, Robert ordered fireworks from China, signal flares from Germany, and flaming arrows from England. When the boxes arrived, he had one burning question: What made these small rockets soar?

He traced their shapes.

He examined each fuse.

And dissected all the explosive ingredients.

Robert researched, designed, and tinkered.

His first rocket was ready to go.

Robert walked to the meadow behind his house and set up for his first launch. After tying a high-flying balloon powered by solar energy to his rocket, Robert watched it lift off. Would this work?

POP!

It fell from the sky. Robert headed back to work.

Month after month, he crafted. He built. He finished rocket
number two.

The new rocket was shaped like a cylinder with a pointed nozzle. He filled it with gunpowder and lit the fuse. Would this work?

BAM!

It exploded.

Determined to figure it out, Robert sat down at his drawing board. He drafted. He framed. He completed his third rocket.

This rocket was shaped like a triangle with fins. He used gasoline to make it fly.

BANG! It crashed and burned.

Year after year, rocket after rocket, Robert wrote in his journal: Cylinder shapes work best. Gunpowder burns too fast. Fins help stability.

And each failure taught Robert something
new. Each failure brought him closer to his dream
of soaring to space.

Still, none of his rockets flew the way he wanted.
Something was missing!

Robert leafed through the pages of his old journals. There it was! In his very first journal was the diamond-explosion entry and the mistake he had made from combining hydrogen, oxygen, and a flame.

Robert had
a whole new
idea for rocket
number four.

On March 16, 1926, a cold day, Robert's newly
built rocket was positioned in the meadow. He held the
release cord. A blowtorch ignited the long fuse that
trailed from the rocket, which was full of hydrogen and
oxygen.

The fuse burned.

The rocket rumbled.

A bright white flame shot from the bottom of the rocket.

The cord released.

The rocket soared.

Mission accomplished.

Robert's extensive rocket research launched the way for every shuttle that has blasted into space, every astronaut who has defied gravity, and every man who has walked on the moon.

All because of a curious boy who discovered how to let sparks fly.

Author's Note

Robert Goddard is considered the father of US rocketry. His March 16, 1926, launch was the world's first successful flight of a liquid-fueled rocket. It reached the height of 41 feet in 2.5 seconds, and it came to rest 184 feet from the launchpad.

Although that particular rocket did not reach space, his March 16 experiment and fuel formula paved the way for space exploration.

Robert passed away in 1945 from cancer. By that time, he had designed and launched over one hundred different rockets. Just a few years later the Soviet Union launched the *Sputnik* satellite and the United States sent the satellite *Explorer 1* into space. By the mid-1960s both countries were sending astronauts into space with rockets fueled by liquid hydrogen and oxygen.

Goddard held 214 patents; many of his inventions and designs were used to create other devices, including:

- NASA's multipart space shuttle (based on the original Goddard rocket)
- Torpedoes (based on a 1914 Goddard rocket design)
- The Swissmetro (designed using one of Goddard's research papers about using airless tunnels)
- Radio transmitters
- The bazooka

To this day, the United States Department of Defense still uses Goddard's designs in building rockets for space exploration.

Works Cited

Clary, David A. *Rocket Man: Robert H. Goddard and the Birth of the Space Age.* New York: Hyperion, 2003. Print.

Curtis, John. "Scientist Seeks Rocket." *Portsmouth Times,* September 21, 1936: 21. Print.

Goddard, Robert H. "Autobiography for Inventor's Bulletin." 1924. MS. Clark University, Goddard Library, Worcester.

_____. "Green Journals." Original ed., 5 vols. Print.

_____. "Red Journals 1924–1939." 1924–1939 10th set. 1 (1924): Print.

_____. "Taking Things for Granted." *Worcester Post* [Worcester, MA], June 24, 1904: Print.

"Goddard Working on Experiment." *Worcester Post* [Worcester, MA.], January 1, 1917: Print.

Haga, Enoch J. "Robert H. Goddard, Father of the Liquid Fuel Rocket." School Science and Mathematics 83.4 (1983): 348-51. Print.

"Invents Rockets with Altitude Range 70 Miles." *Worcester Evening Gazette* [Worcester, MA.] March 28, 1919: Print.

Lehman, Milton. *This High Man; the Life of Robert H. Goddard.* New York: Farrar, Straus, 1963. Print.

Morris, Kathie. "Second Annual Goddard Days." *Roswell Daily Record* [Roswell, New Mexico] October 8, 2000: 25+. Print.

Pendray, G. E. "Robert H. Goddard." *Science* 102.2656 (1945): 521-23. Print.

"Special Robert Goddard Edition." *Roswell Daily Record* [Roswell, New Mexico] March 12, 1999: Print.

Streissguth, Thomas. *Rocket Man: The Story of Robert Goddard.* Minneapolis: Carolrhoda Books, 1995. Print.

United States. Congress. House. Gold Medal Honoring the Late Prof. Robert H. Goddard Report (to Accompany H.R. Res. 19). Washington, DC: US G.P.O., 1959. Print.

United States. Congress. Senate. Goddard Rocket Launching Site and Potomac River Historical Area: Hearing before the Subcommittee on Parks and Recreation of the Committee on Interior and Insular Affairs, United States Senate, Ninety-fourth Congress, Second Session, on S. 397, a Bill to Authorize the Acquisition and Maintenance of the Goddard Rocket Launching Site in Accordance with the Act of August 25, 1916, as Amended and Supplemented, and for Other Purposes; S. 2561, a Bill to Establish the Potomac River Historical Area in the States of Maryland, Virginia and West Virginia, and for Other Purposes, February 24, 1976. Washington: U.S. Govt. Print. Off., 1976. Print.

Winders, Gertrude Hecker. *Robert Goddard, Father of Rocketry.* New York: John Day, 1963. Print.

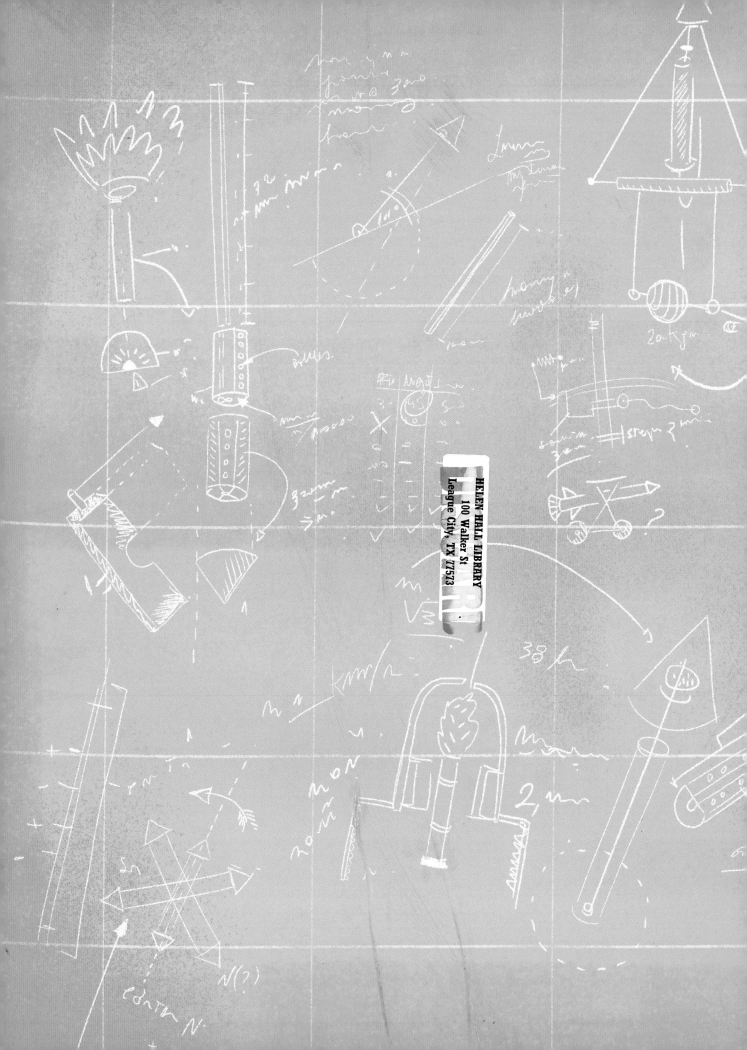